CREATIVE COMPUTING

Learner Workbook

This workbook belongs to:
_____

UNIT 0
GETTING STARTED

YOU ARE HERE

WHAT'S INCLUDED

0   1   2   3   4   5   6

INTRODUCING SCRATCH
SCRATCH ACCOUNT
DESIGN JOURNAL
SCRATCH SURPRISE
SCRATCH STUDIO
CRITIQUE GROUP

clicked

10

10 st...

...ge color... ... effect b... 25

drum 4▼ for 0.2 beats

Welcome to Scratch! for 2

INTRODUCING SCRATCH REFLECTIONS

NAME:

RESPOND TO THE FOLLOWING REFLECTION PROMPTS USING THE SPACE PROVIDED BELOW OR IN YOUR DESIGN JOURNAL.

+ What are the different ways you interact with computers?

+ How many of those ways involve being creative with computers?

SCRATCH ACCOUNT

NEW TO SCRATCH? GET STARTED BY CREATING YOUR SCRATCH ACCOUNT!

You will need a Scratch account to create, save, and share your Scratch projects. The steps below will walk you through creating a new account and setting up your profile.

START HERE

- ❑ Open a web browser and navigate to the Scratch website: http://scratch.mit.edu

- ❑ On the homepage, click on "Join Scratch" at the top on the right or in the blue circle.

- ❑ Complete the three steps to sign up for your very own Scratch account!

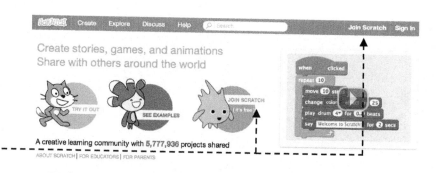

Join Scratch

It's easy (and free!) to sign up for a Scratch account.

Choose a Scratch Username   [   ]   Don't use your real name

Choose a Password

Confirm Password

     2   3   Next

SCRATCH ACCOUNT REFLECTIONS

NAME:

_____

RESPOND TO THE FOLLOWING REFLECTION PROMPTS USING THE SPACE PROVIDED BELOW OR IN YOUR DESIGN JOURNAL.

+ What is your Scratch account username?

+ What is a hint to help you remember your password?

Perry's Design Notebook

DESIGN JOURNAL
REFLECTIONS

NAME:

RESPOND TO THE FOLLOWING REFLECTION PROMPTS USING THE SPACE PROVIDED BELOW OR IN YOUR DESIGN JOURNAL.

+ How would you describe Scratch to a friend?

+ Write or sketch ideas for three different Scratch projects you are interested in creating.

SCRATCH SURPRISE

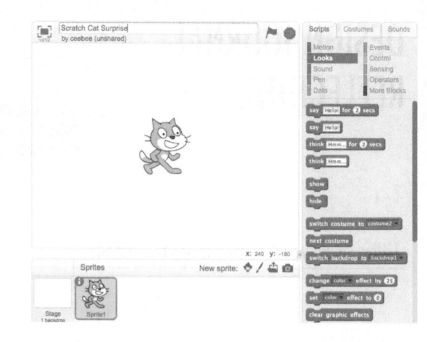

> CAN YOU MAKE THE SCRATCH CAT DO SOMETHING SURPRISING?

In this activity, you will create a new project with Scratch and explore different Scratch blocks to make the cat do something surprising! What will you create? - - - - - - - ►

START HERE

☐ Go to the Scratch website: http://scratch.mit.edu

☐ Sign into your account.

☐ Click on the "Create" tab located at the top left of the browser to start a new project. - - - - - - -

☐ Time to explore! Try clicking on different parts of the Scratch interface to see what happens. - - - - -

☐ Play with different Scratch blocks! Drag and drop Scratch blocks into the scripting area. Experiment by clicking on each block to see what they do or try snapping blocks together. - - - - - -

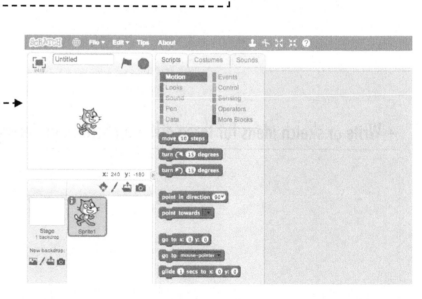

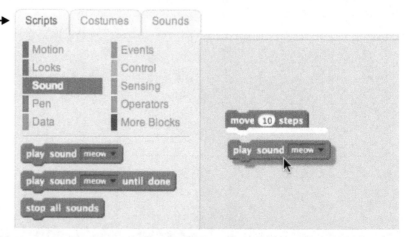

SCRATCH SURPRISE REFLECTIONS

NAME:

RESPOND TO THE FOLLOWING REFLECTION PROMPTS USING THE SPACE PROVIDED BELOW OR IN YOUR DESIGN JOURNAL.

+ What did you figure out?

+ What do you want to know more about?

SCRATCH STUDIO

LEARN HOW TO ADD YOUR PROJECT TO
AN ONLINE SCRATCH STUDIO!

Studios are collections of Scratch projects.
Follow along with the steps below to add
your Scratch Surprise program to the Scratch
Surprise studio on the Scratch website. ------►

START HERE

❑ Go to the Scratch Surprise studio using this link:
   http://scratch.mit.edu/studios/460431 -------►

❑ Sign into your account.

❑ Click on "Add Projects" at the bottom of the page to
   show your your projects, favorite projects, and
   recently viewed projects. -----------

❑ Use the arrows to find your Scratch Surprise project
   and then click "Add + " to add your project to the
   studio.

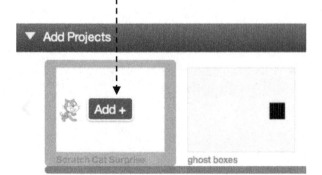

SCRATCH STUDIO REFLECTIONS

NAME: _____

RESPOND TO THE FOLLOWING REFLECTION PROMPTS USING THE SPACE PROVIDED BELOW OR IN YOUR DESIGN JOURNAL.

+ What are Scratch studios for?

+ What did you find interesting or inspiring about looking at other projects?

+ What two comments did you share?

+ What is "good" feedback?

13

CRITIQUE GROUP

FEEDBACK FOR: _____

PROJECT TITLE: _____

FEEDBACK BY	[RED] What is something that doesn't work or could be improved?	[YELLOW] What is something that is confusing or could be done differently?	[GREEN] What is something that works well or you really like about the project?

PARTS OF THE PROJECT THAT MIGHT BE HELPFUL TO THINK ABOUT:

+ Clarity: Did you understand what the project is supposed to do?
+ Features: What features does the project have? Does the project work as expected?
+ Appeal: How engaging is the project? Is it interactive, original, sophisticated, funny, or interesting? How did you feel as you interacted with it?

UNIT 1
EXPLORING

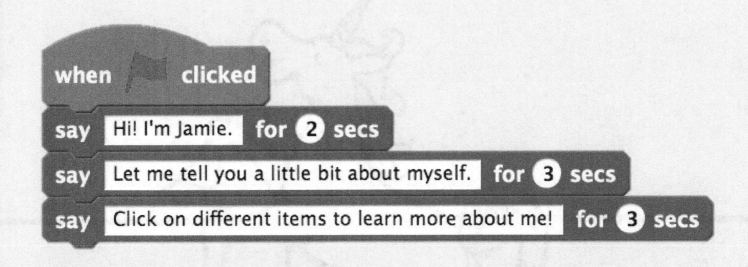

when 🏳 clicked

say Hi! I'm Jamie. for 2 secs

say Let me tell you a little bit about myself. for 3 secs

say Click on different items to learn more about me! for 3 secs

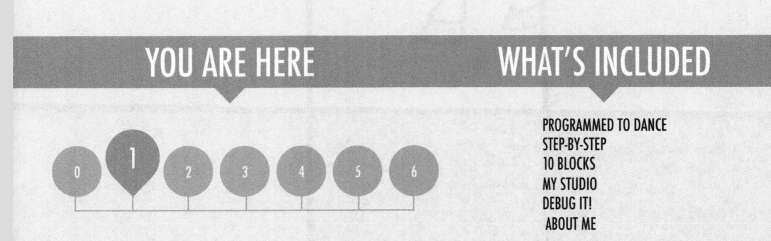

YOU ARE HERE

0 1 2 3 4 5 6

WHAT'S INCLUDED

PROGRAMMED TO DANCE
STEP-BY-STEP
10 BLOCKS
MY STUDIO
DEBUG IT!
ABOUT ME

PROGRAMMED TO DANCE REFLECTIONS

NAME:

RESPOND TO THE FOLLOWING REFLECTION PROMPTS USING THE SPACE PROVIDED BELOW OR IN YOUR DESIGN JOURNAL.

+ What was easy/difficult about being the bossy partner?

+ What was easy/difficult about being the bossed partner?

+ What was easy/difficult about watching?

+ How does this activity relate to what we're doing with Scratch?

19

STEP-BY-STEP

NEW TO SCRATCH? CREATE YOUR FIRST
SCRATCH PROJECT!

In this activity, you will follow the Step-by-Step Intro in the Tips Window to create a dancing cat in Scratch. Once you have completed the steps, experiment by adding other Scratch blocks to make the project your own.

START HERE

- ❑ Follow the Step-by-Step Intro in the Tips Window.
- ❑ Add more blocks.
- ❑ Experiment to make it your own!

turn ↻ 15 degrees

turn ↺ 15 degrees

glide 1 secs to x: ⬤ y: ⬤

change tempo by 20

What blocks do you want to experiment with?

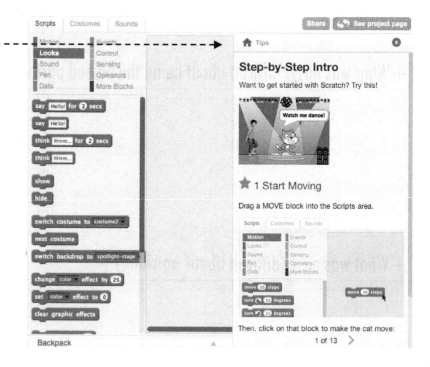

THINGS TO TRY

- ❑ Try recording your own sounds.
- ❑ Create different backdrops.
- ❑ Turn your project into a dance party by adding more dancing sprites!
- ❑ Try designing a new costume for your sprite.

FINISHED?

- + Add your project to the Step-by-Step Studio: http://scratch.mit.edu/studios/475476
- + Challenge yourself to do more! Play with adding new blocks, sound, or motion.
- + Help a neighbor!
- + Choose a few new blocks to experiment with. Try them out!

STEP-BY-STEP REFLECTIONS

NAME:

RESPOND TO THE FOLLOWING REFLECTION PROMPTS USING THE SPACE PROVIDED BELOW OR IN YOUR DESIGN JOURNAL.

+ What was surprising about the activity?

+ How did it feel to be led step-by-step through the activity?

+ When do you feel most creative?

10 BLOCKS

WHAT CAN YOU CREATE WITH ONLY 10 SCRATCH BLOCKS?

Create a project using only these 10 blocks. Use them once, twice, or multiple times, but use each block at least once.

START HERE

❏ Test ideas by experimenting with each block.
❏ Mix and match blocks in various ways.
❏ Repeat!

FEELING STUCK?

THAT'S OKAY! TRY THESE THINGS...

`go to x: 0 y: 0`

`glide 1 secs to x: 0 y: 0`

`say Hello! for 2 secs`

`show`

`hide`

`set size to 100 %`

`play sound meow until done`

`wait 1 secs`

`when this sprite clicked`

`repeat 10`

FINISHED?

❏ Test ideas by trying out different block combinations. Mix and match blocks until you find something that interests you!
❏ Try brainstorming ideas with a neighbor!
❏ Explore other projects to see what others are doing in Scratch. This can be a great way to find inspiration!

+ Add your project to the 10 Blocks Studio: http://scratch.mit.edu/studios/475480
+ Play with different sprites, costumes, or backdrops.
+ Challenge yourself to do more! See how many different projects you can create with these 10 blocks.
+ Swap projects with a partner and remix each others' creations.

10 BLOCKS REFLECTIONS

NAME:

RESPOND TO THE FOLLOWING REFLECTION PROMPTS USING THE SPACE PROVIDED BELOW OR IN YOUR DESIGN JOURNAL.

+ What was difficult about being able to use only 10 blocks?

+ What was easy about being able to use only 10 blocks?

+ How did it make you think of things differently?

MY STUDIO

In this activity, you will investigate the range of creative possibility with Scratch by exploring some of the millions of projects on the Scratch website – and start a collection of favorites in a Scratch studio! - - - - - - - - - ➤

My Studio

| Projects (4) | Comments (0) | Curator |

Report this studio

Updated 28 May 2013
My studio of interesting projects.

Full 16 Frame Scratch ...
by griffpatch

Automatic Drawing
by ScratchEdTeam

Slideshow
by ScratchEdTeam

NiavL
by CastillejaSTEM

START HERE

- ☐ Browse projects on the Scratch homepage OR click on "Explore" to search for specific types of projects. - - - -
- ☐ Create a new studio from your My Stuff page.
- ☐ Add three (or more!) inspiring projects to your studio.

Create stories, games, and animations
Share with others around the world

A creative learning community with 5,671,545 projects shared

ABOUT SCRATCH | FOR EDUCATORS | FOR PARENTS

Featured Projects

Scratch's SINGATHON!
by helloyowuzzup

Simple Angle Calculator
by junebeetle

Escape
by devindubos

FINISHED Rainbowdas...
by 2009312

Matoran
by GoldenMiru

Featured Studios

THINGS TO TRY

- ☐ Use the search bar to find projects that relate to your interests.
- ☐ Explore each of the Animations, Art, Games, Music, & Stories categories on the Explore page.
- ☐ Look through the Featured Studios on the homepage for ideas.

FINISHED?

- + Challenge yourself to do more! The more Scratch projects you explore, the more you learn about what can be accomplished in Scratch!
- + Find studios created by other Scratchers that you find interesting!
- + Ask a neighbor what strategies they used to find interesting projects.
- + Share your newly created studio with a neighbor!

MY STUDIO REFLECTIONS

NAME:

RESPOND TO THE FOLLOWING REFLECTION PROMPTS USING THE SPACE PROVIDED BELOW OR IN YOUR DESIGN JOURNAL.

+ What search strategies did you use to find interesting projects?

+ How might each example project help with future work?

+ It's important to give credit to sources of inspiration.
  How can you give credit for inspiration from these projects?

25

DEBUG IT!

HELP! CAN YOU DEBUG THESE FIVE SCRATCH PROGRAMS?

In this activity, you will investigate what is going awry and find a solution for each of the five Debug It! challenges.

START HERE

❏ Go to the Unit 1 Debug It! studio:
http://scratch.mit.edu/studios/475483

❏ Test and debug each of the five debugging challenges in the studio.

❏ Write down your solution or remix the buggy program with your solution.

FEELING STUCK?

THAT'S OKAY! TRY THESE THINGS...

❏ Make a list of possible bugs in the program.

❏ Keep track of your work! This can be a useful reminder of what you have already tried and point you toward what to try next.

❏ Share and compare your problem finding and problem solving approaches with a neighbor until you find something that works for you!

❏ **DEBUG IT! 1.1** http://scratch.mit.edu/projects/10437040

When the green flag is clicked, both Gobo and Scratch Cat should start dancing. But only Scratch Cat starts Dancing! How do we fix the program?

❏ **DEBUG IT! 1.2** http://scratch.mit.edu/projects/10437249

In this project, when the green flag is clicked, the Scratch Cat should start on the left side of the stage, say something about being on the left side, glide to the right side of the stage, and say something about being on the right side. It works the first time the green flag is clicked, but not again. How do we fix the program?

❏ **DEBUG IT! 1.3** http://scratch.mit.edu/projects/10437366

The Scratch Cat should do a flip when the space key is pressed. But when the space key is pressed, nothing happens! How do we fix the program?

❏ **DEBUG IT! 1.4** http://scratch.mit.edu/projects/10437439

In this project, the Scratch Cat should pace back and forth across the stage, when it is clicked. But the Scratch Cat is flipping out – and is walking upside down! How do we fix the program?

❏ **DEBUG IT! 1.5** http://scratch.mit.edu/projects/10437476

In this project, when the green flag is clicked, the Scratch Cat should saw 'Meow, meow, meow!' in a speech bubble and as a sound. But the speech bubble happens before the sound – and the Scratch Cat only makes one 'Meow' sound! How do we fix the program?

FINISHED?

+ Discuss your testing and debugging practices with a partner. Make note of the similarities and differences in your strategies.

+ Add code commentary by right clicking on blocks in your scripts. This can help others understand different parts of your program!

+ Help a neighbor!

DEBUG IT!
REFLECTIONS

NAME:

RESPOND TO THE FOLLOWING REFLECTION PROMPTS USING THE SPACE PROVIDED BELOW OR IN YOUR DESIGN JOURNAL.

+ What was the problem?

+ How did you identify the problem?

+ How did you fix the problem?

+ Did others have alternative approaches to fixing the problem?

ABOUT ME

HOW CAN YOU COMBINE INTERESTING IMAGES AND SOUNDS TO MAKE AN INTERACTIVE COLLAGE ABOUT YOURSELF?

Experiment with sprites, costumes, backdrops, looks, and sounds to create an interactive Scratch project – a project that helps other people learn more about YOU and the ideas, activities, and people that you care about.

Click on different items to learn more about me.

START HERE

☐ Create a sprite.
☐ Make it interactive.
☐ Repeat!

```
when this sprite clicked
play sound whoop ▼ until done
```

```
when this sprite clicked
repeat 10
  turn ↻ 15 degrees
  wait .3 secs
  turn ↺ 15 degrees
  wait .3 secs
```

Make your sprite interactive by adding scripts that have the sprite respond to clicks, key presses, and more!

Sprites   New sprite: ◆ / ⬆ 📷

Stage
1 backdrop

New backdrop:
🖼 / ⬆ 📷

Sprite1

THINGS TO TRY

☐ Use costumes to change how your sprite looks.
☐ Create different backdrops.
☐ Try adding sound to your project.
☐ Try adding movement into your collage.

BLOCKS TO PLAY WITH

```
when ▢ clicked
```
```
when this sprite clicked
```
```
when space ▼ key pressed
```

```
move 10 steps
```
```
go to x: 0 y: 0
```
```
glide 1 secs to x: 0 y: 0
```
```
say Hello! for 2 secs
```

```
change color ▼ effect by 25
```
```
change size by 10
```
```
show    hide
```
```
play sound meow ▼ until done
```

```
wait 1 secs
```
```
repeat 10
```
```
forever
```

FINISHED?

+ Add your project to the About Me Studio: http://scratch.mit.edu/studios/475470
+ Challenge yourself to do more! Play with adding new blocks, sound, or motion!
+ Help a neighbor!

ABOUT ME
REFLECTIONS

NAME:

RESPOND TO THE FOLLOWING REFLECTION PROMPTS USING THE SPACE PROVIDED BELOW OR IN YOUR DESIGN JOURNAL.

+ What are you most proud of? Why?

+ What did you get stuck on? How did you get unstuck?

+ What might you want to do next?

+ What did you discover from looking at others' About Me projects?

UNIT 2
ANIMATIONS

Turn up the music!

YOU ARE HERE

0 1 **2** 3 4 5 6

WHAT'S INCLUDED

PERFORMING SCRIPTS
BUILD-A-BAND
ORANGE SQUARE, PURPLE CIRCLE
IT'S ALIVE!
DEBUG IT!
MUSIC VIDEO

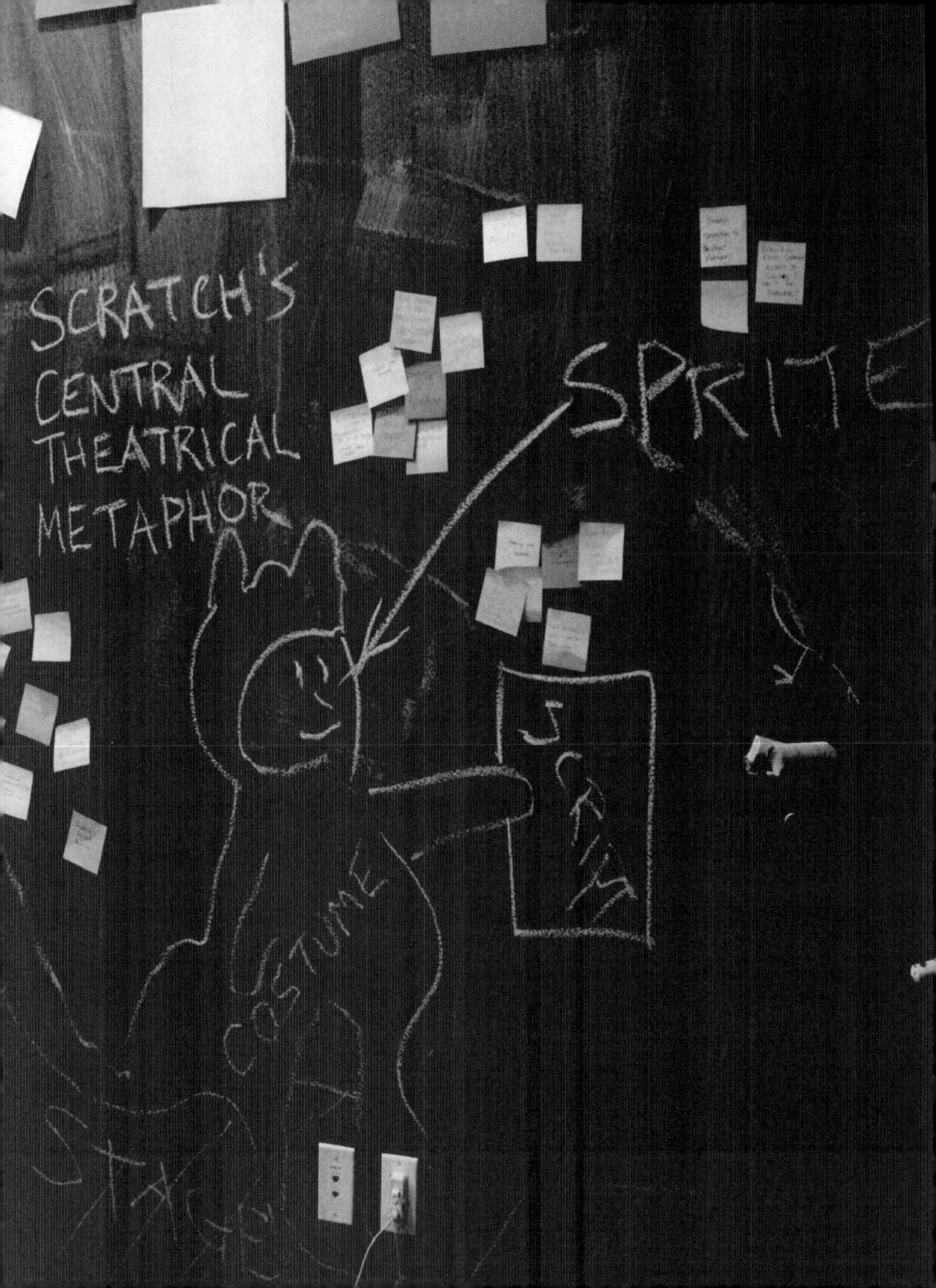
SCRATCH'S
CENTRAL
THEATRICAL
METAPHOR
SPRITE
COSTUME

PERFORMING SCRIPTS REFLECTIONS

NAME:

RESPOND TO THE FOLLOWING REFLECTION PROMPTS USING THE SPACE PROVIDED BELOW OR IN YOUR DESIGN JOURNAL.

+ What are the different ways that actions were triggered?

+ What are the mechanisms for events in Scratch?

+ What were the different ways in which things were happening at the same time?

+ What are the mechanisms that enable parallelism in Scratch?

BUILD-A-BAND

HOW CAN YOU UTILIZE SCRATCH TO CREATE SOUNDS, INSTRUMENTS, BANDS, OR STYLES OF MUSIC THAT REPRESENT THE MUSIC YOU LOVE MOST?

In this activity, you will build your own music-inspired Scratch project by pairing sprites with sounds to design interactive instruments.

START HERE

❏ Create a sprite.
❏ Add sound blocks.
❏ Experiment with ways to make your instruments interactive.

Choose instruments from the sprite library or create your own.

```
when this sprite clicked
repeat 10
    play drum 6▾ for .2 beats
    rest for 0.2 beats
```

```
when this sprite clicked
repeat 8
    play drum 8▾ for .2 beats
    wait 1 secs
```

```
when this sprite clicked
repeat 10
    play drum 2▾ for .5 beats
    play drum 1▾ for .5 beats
```

THINGS TO TRY

❏ Use repeat blocks to make a sound play more than once.
❏ Import or record your own sounds or experiment with the Sounds editor.
❏ Try playing with the tempo blocks to speed up or slow down the rhythm.

FINISHED?

+ Add your project to the Build-A-Band Studio: http://scratch.mit.edu/studios/475523
+ Challenge yourself to do more! Invent a new instrument or record your own sounds.
+ Help a neighbor!

BUILD-A-BAND REFLECTIONS

NAME:

RESPOND TO THE FOLLOWING REFLECTION PROMPTS USING THE SPACE PROVIDED BELOW OR IN YOUR DESIGN JOURNAL.

+ What did you do first?

+ What did you do next?

+ What did you do last?

ORANGE SQUARE, PURPLE CIRCLE

WHAT PROJECT CAN YOU CREATE THAT INCLUDES AN ORANGE SQUARE AND A PURPLE CIRCLE?

In this challenge, you'll create a project that includes an orange square and a purple circle. What will you create? - - - - - - - - - - - - ->

START HERE

❏ Draw your sprites using the Paint Editor. - - - - - - - -
❏ Add different Looks and Motion blocks to bring your
   sprites to life. - - - - - - - - - - - - - - -
❏ Repeat!

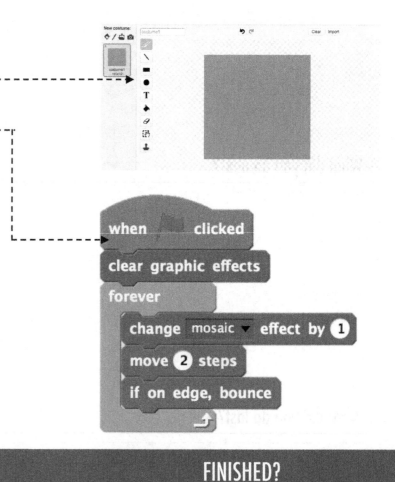

FEELING STUCK?

THAT'S OKAY! TRY THESE THINGS...

❏ Try brainstorming with a neighbor!
❏ Create a list of things you would like to try before you start building your project in Scratch!
❏ Explore other projects to see what others are doing in Scratch - this can be a great way to find inspiration!

FINISHED?

+ Add your project to the Orange Square, Purple Circle Studio: http://scratch.mit.edu/studios/475527
+ Explore the difference between bitmap mode and vector mode, located at the bottom of the paint editor.
+ Challenge yourself to do more! Add another shape and color.
+ Swap projects with a partner and remix each other's creations.
+ Help a neighbor!

ORANGE SQUARE, PURPLE CIRCLE REFLECTIONS

NAME:

RESPOND TO THE FOLLOWING REFLECTION PROMPTS USING THE SPACE PROVIDED BELOW OR IN YOUR DESIGN JOURNAL.

+ How did you incorporate an orange square and a purple circle into your project? Where did this idea come from?

+ What was challenging about this activity?

+ What was surprising about this activity?

IT'S ALIVE!

HOW CAN YOU TAKE AN IMAGE OR A
PHOTO AND MAKE IT COME ALIVE?

In this activity, you will explore ways of
bringing sprites, images, and ideas to life as
an animation by programming a series of
costume changes.

START HERE

❏ Choose a sprite.
❏ Add a different costume.
❏ Add blocks to make the image come alive.
❏ Repeat!

```
when this sprite clicked
repeat 10
    wait .1 secs
    move 10 steps
    next costume
```

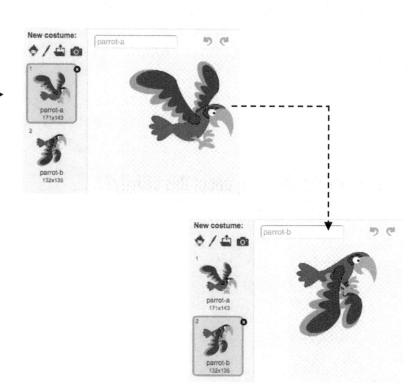

THINGS TO TRY

❏ Try sketching your animation ideas on
paper first – like a flipbook.
❏ Experiment with different blocks and
costumes until you find something you
enjoy.
❏ Need some inspiration? Find projects in the
Animation section of the Explore page.

FINISHED?

+ Add your project to the It's Alive studio: http://scratch.mit.edu/studios/475529
+ Challenge yourself to do more! Add more features to your project to make your
animations look even more lifelike.
+ Help a neighbor!
+ Share your project with a partner and walk them through your design process.
+ Find an animated project you're inspired by and remix it!

IT'S ALIVE!
REFLECTIONS

NAME:

RESPOND TO THE FOLLOWING REFLECTION PROMPTS USING THE SPACE PROVIDED BELOW OR IN YOUR DESIGN JOURNAL.

+ What is the difference between a sprite and a costume?

+ What is an animation?

+ List three ways you experience loops in real life (e.g., going to sleep every night).

DEBUG IT!

HELP! CAN YOU DEBUG THESE FIVE SCRATCH PROGRAMS?

In this activity, you will investigate what is going awry and find a solution for each of the five Debug It! challenges.

START HERE

- ❑ Go to the Unit 2 Debug It! Studio:
  http://scratch.mit.edu/studios/475539
- ❑ Test and debug each of the five debugging challenges in the studio.
- ❑ Write down your solution or remix the buggy program with your solution.

FEELING STUCK?

THAT'S OKAY! TRY THESE THINGS...

❑ **DEBUG IT! 2.1** http://scratch.mit.edu/projects/23266426

In this project, Scratch Cat wants to show you a dance. When you click on him, he should do a dance while a drum beat plays along with him. However, as soon as he starts to dance he stops but the drumming continues without him! How do we fix this program?

❑ **DEBUG IT! 2.2** http://scratch.mit.edu/projects/24268476

In this project, when the green flag is clicked Pico should move towards Nano. When Pico reaches Nano, Pico should say "Tag, you're it!" and Nano says "My turn!" But something is wrong! Pico doesn't say anything to Nano. How do we fix the program?

❑ **DEBUG IT! 2.3** http://scratch.mit.edu/projects/24268506

This project is programmed to draw a happy face but something is not quite right! The pen continues to draw from one of the eyes to the smile when it should not be doing so. How do we fix the program?

❑ **DEBUG IT! 2.4** http://scratch.mit.edu/projects/23267140

In this project, when the green flag is clicked an animation of a flower growing begins and stops once it has fully bloomed. But something is not quite right! Instead of stopping when all the petals have bloomed, the animation starts all over. How do we fix this program?

❑ **DEBUG IT! 2.5** http://scratch.mit.edu/projects/23267245

In this project, the Happy Birthday song starts playing when the green flag is clicked. Once the song finishes, instructions should appear telling us to "click on me to blow out the candles!" But something is not working! The instructions to blow out the candles are shown while the birthday song is playing rather than after it finishes. How do we fix this program?

FINISHED?

- ❑ Make a list of possible bugs in the program.
- ❑ Keep track of your work! This can be a useful reminder of what you have already tried and point you toward what to try next.
- ❑ Share and compare your problem finding and problem solving approaches with a neighbor until you find something that works for you!

- + Add code commentary by right clicking on blocks in your scripts. This can help others understand different parts of your program!
- + Discuss your testing and debugging practices with a partner - make notes of the similarities and differences in your strategies.
- + Help a neighbor!

DEBUG IT!
REFLECTIONS

NAME:

RESPOND TO THE FOLLOWING REFLECTION PROMPTS USING THE SPACE PROVIDED BELOW OR IN YOUR DESIGN JOURNAL.

+ What was the problem?

+ How did you identify the problem?

+ How did you fix the problem?

+ Did others have alternative approaches to fixing the problem?

MUSIC VIDEO

HOW CAN YOU COMBINE ANIMATION WITH MUSIC TO CREATE YOUR OWN SCRATCH-INSPIRED MUSIC VIDEO?

In this project, you will explore ideas related to theatre, song, dance, music, drawing, illustration, photography, and animation to create a personalized music video! - - - - - - - - ▶

START HERE

❑ Add sound. -
❑ Create and animate a sprite. - - - - - - - - - - - - - - -
❑ Make them interact together!

```
when this sprite clicked
change  whirl ▾  effect by  -50
play drum  2▾  for  .5  beats
change  whirl ▾  effect by  50
play drum  8▾  for  .5  beats
switch costume to  cassy-dancing-1 ▾
play drum  2▾  for  0.125  beats
turn  ↻  15  degrees
play drum  6▾  for  0.25  beats
turn  ↺  15  degrees
play drum  2▾  for  .25  beats
switch costume to  cassy-dancing-2 ▾
play drum  8▾  for  .5  beats
```

| Scripts | Costumes | **Sounds** |

New sound:
🔊 🎤 📤 - - ▶ upload sounds from a file
record your own sounds
choose sounds from library

New sprite: 🐱 🖌 📤 📷
choose sprite from library
paint your own sprite
upload sprite from file
new sprite from camera

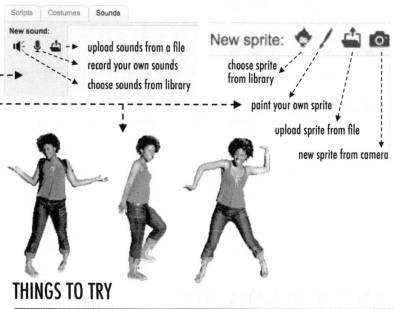

THINGS TO TRY

❑ Use costumes to help bring your animations to life!
❑ Make your sprite interactive by adding scripts that have the sprite respond to clicks, key presses, and more.
❑ Add instructions on the project page to explain how people can interact with your program.

BLOCKS TO PLAY WITH

```
when      clicked
```
```
when this sprite clicked
```
```
when  space ▾  key pressed
```

```
turn  ↻  15  degrees
```
```
turn  ↺  15  degrees
```
```
if on edge, bounce
```
```
rest for  0.25  beats
```

```
switch costume to  costume1 ▾
```
```
next costume        costume #
```
```
switch backdrop to  backdrop1 ▾
```
```
play drum  1▾  for  0.25  beats
```

```
wait  1  secs
```
```
repeat  10
```
```
forever
```

FINISHED?

+ Add your project to the Music Video studio: http://scratch.mit.edu/studios/475517

+ Be sure to give credit to any music, cod or other work used in your project.

+ Challenge yourself to do more! Create your own sprites, sounds, or costumes!

42

MUSIC VIDEO REFLECTIONS

NAME:

RESPOND TO THE FOLLOWING REFLECTION PROMPTS USING THE SPACE PROVIDED BELOW OR IN YOUR DESIGN JOURNAL.

+ What was a challenge you overcame? How did you overcome it?

+ What is something you still want to figure out?

+ How did you give credit for ideas, music, or code that you borrowed to use in your project?

UNIT 3
STORIES

YOU ARE HERE

WHAT'S INCLUDED

0   1   2   **3**   4   5   6

CONVERSATIONS
SCENES
DEBUG IT!
CREATURE CONSTRUCTION
PASS IT ON

CHARACTERS

DO YOU WANT TO CREATE YOUR OWN SCRATCH BLOCKS?

Experiment with the Make a Block feature in Scratch! In this project, you will create your own blocks that define two behaviors for two different characters.

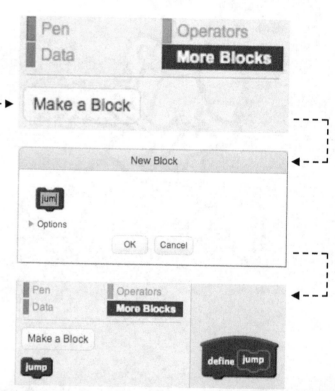

Press S for a small jump.
Press B for a big jump
Press A to ask how high to jump.

START HERE

☐ Choose from the library, paint, or upload two sprite characters.

☐ Click on the Make a Block button in the More Blocks category to create and name your block.

☐ Add blocks under the Define block to control what your custom block will do.

☐ Experiment with using your block to program your characters' behaviors.

☐ Repeat!

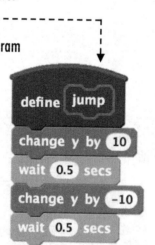

THINGS TO TRY

☐ Feeling stuck? That's okay! Check out this video to get started with the Make a Block feature: http://bit.ly/makeablock

☐ Explore other projects in the Characters Studio to see what new blocks others have created.

☐ Sometimes there can be more than one way of defining the same behavior. Experiment with different block combinations to try out multiple options and outcomes.

FINISHED?

+ Add your project to the Characters Studio: http://scratch.mit.edu/studios/475545

+ Challenge yourself to do more! Experiment with adding different characters and behaviors using the Make a Block feature.

+ Help a neighbor!

CHARACTERS REFLECTIONS

NAME:

RESPOND TO THE FOLLOWING REFLECTION PROMPTS USING THE SPACE PROVIDED BELOW OR IN YOUR DESIGN JOURNAL.

+ How would you explain Make a Block to someone else?

+ When might you use Make a Block?

CONVERSATIONS

WHAT ARE DIFFERENT WAYS TO COORDINATE INTERACTIONS BETWEEN SPRITES?

In this activity, you'll explore different ways to program sprites to have conversations! Experiment with timing and explore using broadcast by remixing a joke project.

What other jokes do you have?

START HERE

☐ Look inside the Penguin Jokes project:
http://scratch.mit.edu/projects/10015800
☐ Investigate the code to see how the wait and say blocks are used to coordinate the conversation. - - - - - - - - →
☐ Remix the project to use the broadcast and when I receive blocks instead of wait blocks. - - - - -

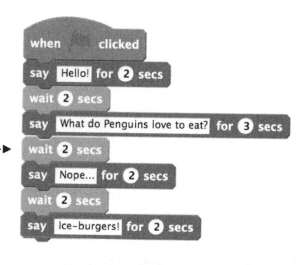

FEELING STUCK?

THAT'S OKAY! TRY THESE THINGS...

FINISHED?

☐ Brainstorm ideas with a neighbor! Generate a list of possible solutions and test them out together.
☐ Try using the broadcast and when I receive blocks in different parts of your project.
☐ Explore projects in the Conversations studio to get inspiration for different ways to coordinate conversations between sprites.

+ Add your project to the Conversations studio:
http://scratch.mit.edu/studios/475547
+ Challenge yourself to do more! Add other characters and conversations.
+ Share your project with a neighbor and walk them through your process of exploration and design.
+ Help a neighbor!

CONVERSATIONS REFLECTIONS

NAME:
_____

RESPOND TO THE FOLLOWING REFLECTION PROMPTS USING THE SPACE PROVIDED BELOW OR IN YOUR DESIGN JOURNAL.

+ How would you describe broadcast to someone else?

+ When would you use timing in a project? When would you use broadcasting?

SCENES

WHAT IS THE DIFFERENCE BETWEEN THE STAGE AND SPRITES?

In this activity, you will create a project that experiments with backdrops, like a story with multiple scenes or a slideshow.

START HERE

❑ Choose from the library, paint, or upload multiple backdrops into your project.

❑ Experiment with blocks from the Looks and Events categories to initiate switching backdrops.

❑ Add scripts to the stage and sprites to coordinate what happens when the backdrop changes in your project!

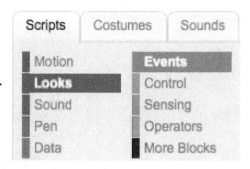

switch backdrop to backdrop1 ▼

when backdrop switches to backdrop1 ▼

backdrop name

THINGS TO TRY

❑ Look for blocks under the sprites and the stage related to backdrop and test them out to see what they do!

❑ Need more inspiration? Explore the Scratch online community to discover projects that use multiple backdrops.

FINISHED?

+ Add your project to the Scenes Studio: http://scratch.mit.edu/studios/475550
+ Challenge yourself to do more! Add more backdrop changes to your project.
+ Help a neighbor!
+ Return to one of your previous projects or find a project you are inspired by and remix it by adding switching backdrops.

SCENES REFLECTIONS

NAME:

RESPOND TO THE FOLLOWING REFLECTION PROMPTS USING THE SPACE PROVIDED BELOW OR IN YOUR DESIGN JOURNAL.

+ What does the Stage have in common with sprites?

+ How is the Stage different from sprites?

+ How do you initiate a sprite's actions in a scene?

+ What other types of projects (beyond animations) use scene changes?

DEBUG IT!

HELP! CAN YOU DEBUG THESE FIVE SCRATCH PROGRAMS?

In this activity, you will investigate what is going awry and find a solution for each of the five Debug It! challenges.

START HERE

- ❏ Go to the Unit 3 Debug It! Studio:
  http://scratch.mit.edu/studios/475554
- ❏ Test and debug each of the five debugging challenges in the studio.
- ❏ Write down your solution or remix the buggy program with your solution.

FEELING STUCK?

THAT'S OKAY! TRY THESE THINGS...

- ❏ Make a list of possible bugs in the program.
- ❏ Keep track of your work! This can be a useful reminder of what you have already tried and point you toward what to try next.
- ❏ Share and compare your problem finding and problem solving approaches with a neighbor until you find something that works for you!

❏ **DEBUG IT! 3.1** http://scratch.mit.edu/projects/24269007

In this project, the Scratch Cat teaches Gobo to meow. But when it's Gobo's turn to try – Gobo stays silent. How do we fix the program?

❏ **DEBUG IT! 3.2** http://scratch.mit.edu/projects/24269046

In this project, the Scratch Cat is supposed to count from 1 to the number the user provides. But the Scratch Cat always counts to 10. How do we fix the program?

❏ **DEBUG IT! 3.3** http://scratch.mit.edu/projects/24269070

In this project, the Scratch Cat is doing roll call with Gobo's friends: Giga, Nano, Pico, and Tera. But everything is happening all at once! How do we fix the program?

❏ **DEBUG IT! 3.4** http://scratch.mit.edu/projects/24269097

In this project, the Scratch Cat and Gobo are practicing their jumping routine. When Scratch Cat says "Jump!", Gobo should jump up and down. But Gobo isn't jumping. How do we fix the program?

❏ **DEBUG IT! 3.5** http://scratch.mit.edu/projects/24269131

In this project, the scene changes when you press the right arrow key. The star of the project – a dinosaur – should be hidden in every scene except when the scene transitions to the auditorium backdrop. In the auditorium, the dinosaur should appear and do a dance. But the dinosaur is always present and is not dancing at the right time. How do we fix the program?

FINISHED?

- + Add code commentary by right clicking on blocks in your scripts. This can help others understand different parts of your program!
- + Discuss your testing and debugging practices with a partner, and make note of the similarities and differences in your strategies.
- + Help a neighbor!

DEBUG IT!
REFLECTIONS

NAME:

RESPOND TO THE FOLLOWING REFLECTION PROMPTS USING THE SPACE PROVIDED BELOW OR IN YOUR DESIGN JOURNAL.

+ What was the problem?

+ How did you identify the problem?

+ How did you fix the problem?

+ Did others have alternative approaches to fixing the problem?

CREATURE CONSTRUCTION REFLECTIONS

NAME:

RESPOND TO THE FOLLOWING REFLECTION PROMPTS USING THE SPACE PROVIDED BELOW OR IN YOUR DESIGN JOURNAL.

+ What is your definition of remixing?

+ Think about the creature you started (drew the "head" for). How did your ideas become extended or enhanced by others' contributions?

+ Considering the creatures you extended (drew the "middle" or "bottom" sections for), how did your contributions extend or enhance others' ideas?

55

PASS IT ON

WHAT CAN WE CREATE BY BUILDING ON OTHERS' WORK?

In this project, you will start developing an animated story project, and then you will pass the story on to others to remix, extend, or reimagine!

START HERE

- ☐ Work on a story project that focuses on characters, scene, plot, or whatever element excites you.
- ☐ After 10 minutes, save and share your project online.
- ☐ Rotate & extend another story project by remixing it.
- ☐ Repeat!

```
when backdrop switches to Title Screen
hide

when [flag] clicked
show

when this sprite clicked
broadcast next page
```

```
when backdrop switches to metro1
set size to 200 %
play sound dog2
glide 1 secs to x: -102 y: -99
glide 1 secs to x: -55 y: -67
glide 1 secs to x: 30 y: -102
```

THINGS TO TRY

- ☐ Brainstorm different possibilities for remixing, extending, or reimagining a story. Do you want to add a new scene to the end? Could you imagine what happens before the story begins? What if a new character was added? How about inserting a plot twist? What else?

- ☐ Adding comments in your code can help others understand different parts of your program. To attach a comment to a script, right click on a block and add a description.

```
when this sprite clicked
broadcast next page
```
add comment here...

BLOCKS TO PLAY WITH

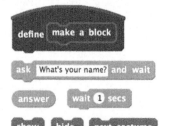

```
when [flag] clicked

when I receive message1

broadcast message1

broadcast message1 and wait
```

```
define make a block

ask What's your name? and wait

answer      wait 1 secs

show   hide   next costume
```

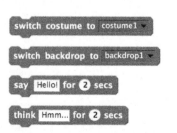

```
switch costume to costume1

switch backdrop to backdrop1

say Hello! for 2 secs

think Hmm... for 2 secs
```

FINISHED?

- + Add your project to the Pass It On studio: http://scratch.mit.edu/studios/475543
- + Help a neighbor!
- + Return to all the projects you contributed to and check out how the stories evolved!

PASS IT ON
REFLECTIONS

NAME:

RESPOND TO THE FOLLOWING REFLECTION PROMPTS USING THE SPACE PROVIDED BELOW OR IN YOUR DESIGN JOURNAL.

+ How did it feel to remix and build on others' work? How did it feel to be remixed?

+ Where else in your life have you seen or experienced reusing and remixing? Share two examples.

+ How was working with someone else different from your prior experiences of designing your Scratch projects?

UNIT 4
GAMES

YOU ARE HERE

0   1   2   3   **4**   5   6

WHAT'S INCLUDED

DREAM GAME LIST
STARTER GAMES
SCORE
EXTENSIONS
INTERACTIONS
DEBUG IT!

Chess

Monopoly

Mario

Clue

Football

Candyland

Pac Man

Jump Rope

Baseball

Tennis

Flappy Bird

Wheel of Fortune

Four Square

DREAM GAME LIST REFLECTIONS

NAME:

RESPOND TO THE FOLLOWING REFLECTION PROMPTS USING THE SPACE PROVIDED BELOW OR IN YOUR DESIGN JOURNAL.

+ Make a list of your favorite games.

+ What do the games have in common?

+ What features of their design make them a game?

+ Create a list of design elements for your dream game.

MAZE

HOW CAN YOU USE SCRATCH TO BUILD AN INTERACTIVE GAME?

In this project, you will create a game. This game includes interactions between sprites, score, and levels. You move a sprite from the start of a maze to the end without touching the walls.

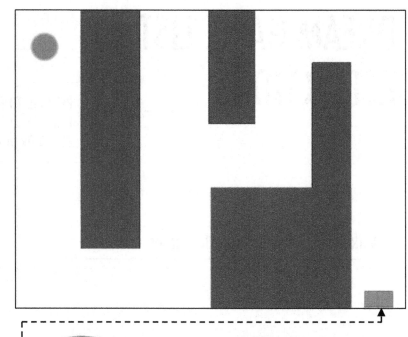

START HERE

❏ Draw a maze-like background and use different colors for the walls and end-of-maze marker.

❏ Add a sprite.

❏ Make your game interactive!

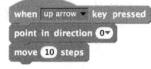

These scripts give the player control over sprite movement in the maze.

This tells your sprite where to begin and marks the start of the maze.

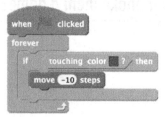

This will cause your sprite to bounce off the blue walls of the maze.

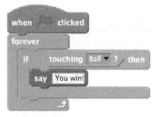

This tells the end-of-maze sprite that players win when the ball touches this sprite.

THINGS TO TRY

❏ Add multiple levels to your game! This can be done through the use of different backdrops and using braodcast blocks to trigger the next level.

❏ Use the make a variable block to keep score!

❏ Experiment with timer blocks to add new challenges to your maze!

BLOCKS TO PLAY WITH

FINISHED?

+ Add your project to the Games Studio: http://scratch.mit.edu/ studios/487504

+ Swap games with a partner and walk each other through your creations.

62

PONG

HOW CAN YOU USE SCRATCH TO BUILD
AN INTERACTIVE GAME?

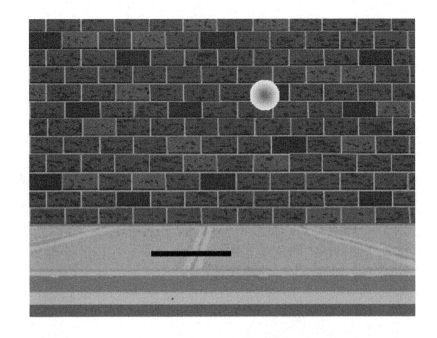

In this project, you will create a game. This
game includes interactions between sprites,
score, and levels. The game is similar to the
classic game of pong, where the goal is to
keep the sprite from getting past you. - - - - - ►

START HERE

☐ Create two sprites: a paddle for the user to control
   and a ball the user will be playing with.

☐ Make your paddle sprite interactive. - - - - - - - - - - - -

☐ Bring your game to life! - - - - - - - - -

Sprites

Ball   Paddle

```
when right arrow key pressed
point in direction 90
move 10 steps
```

```
when left arrow key pressed
point in direction -90
move 10 steps
```

THINGS TO TRY

☐ How do you add difficulty to your game?
   Creating different levels, using a timer, or
   keeping score are a few examples of things you
   could do.

☐ Experiment with changing the look of your game
   by editing the backdrops!

☐ Explore using different key presses to control
   your sprites!

```
when clicked
forever
  if touching Paddle ? then
    play sound water_drop
    turn ↻ pick random 160 to 200 degrees
    move 10 steps
  if touching color ? then
    stop all
```

```
when clicked
go to x: 20 y: 150
point in direction 45
forever
  if on edge, bounce
  move 10 steps
```

- - - Interacts with the walls
- - - - - - - - - Interacts with the paddle

These control the ball - if touching the paddle or a wall, it continues moving. If
touching red (meaning the ball moved past the paddle) the game ends.

BLOCKS TO PLAY WITH

```
when space key pressed

when up arrow key pressed

when m key pressed

when I receive message1
```

```
score

set score to 0

change score by 1

show variable score

hide variable score
```

```
( - )   ( + )

< =

> not

and

or
```

```
pick random 1 to 10

touching ▾ ?

touching color ?

color is touching ?

timer    reset timer
```

FINISHED?

+ Add your project to the Games
  Studio: http://scratch.mit.edu/
  studios/487504

+ Swap games with a partner
  and walk each other through
  your creations.

63

SCROLLING

HOW CAN YOU USE SCRATCH TO BUILD
AN INTERACTIVE GAME?

In this project, you will create a game. This game includes interactions between sprites, score, and levels. The game is similar to Flappy Bird, where the goal is to keep an object from falling to the ground or touching certain objects. - - - - - - - - - - - - - ►

START HERE

❑ Create two sprites: one for the player to control (helicopter) and one to avoid (gliding bars).

❑ Make the helicopter interactive. - ►

❑ Bring your game to life by adding scripts to make the gliding bars scroll across the stage! - - - - - - - ►

Sprites

Gliding bars   Helicopter

THINGS TO TRY

❑ How do you add difficulty to your game? Creating different levels, using a timer, or keeping score are a few examples of things you could do.

❑ Experiment with changing the look of your game by editing the backdrops!

❑ Explore using different key presses to control your sprites!

```
when      clicked
hide
forever
    wait 5 secs
    create clone of myself
```

This creates clones, which are used in the script below to make the bars scroll across the screen:

```
when I start as a clone
switch costume to pick random 1 to 3
go to x: 240 y: 0
show
glide 8 secs to x: -240 y: 0
delete this clone
```

```
when space key pressed
change y by 20
```
Controls sprite movement

```
when      clicked
go to x: 0 y: 0
set size to 30 %
wait 2 secs
forever
    change y by -2
```
Causes sprite to constantly fall downward

```
when      clicked
forever
    if    touching color  ? then
        stop all
```
Specifies when the game ends

BLOCKS TO PLAY WITH

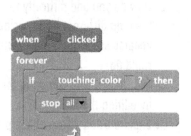

FINISHED?

+ Add your project to the Games Studio: http://scratch.mit.edu/studios/487504

+ Swap games with a partner and walk each other through your creations.

64

STARTER GAMES REFLECTIONS

NAME:

RESPOND TO THE FOLLOWING REFLECTION PROMPTS USING THE SPACE PROVIDED BELOW OR IN YOUR DESIGN JOURNAL.

+ What was challenging about designing your game?

+ What are you proud of?

SCORE

HOW CAN YOU KEEP SCORE IN A SCRATCH PROJECT?

Fish Chomp is a game where players try to catch as many fish as they can by guiding a sprite with the mouse. In this activity, you will remix Fish Chomp by adding a score with variables.

START HERE

- ☐ Go to the Fish Chomp project page: http://scratch.mit.edu/projects/10859244
- ☐ Click on the Make a Variable button in the Data category to create and name a variable for score.
- ☐ Experiment with your new variable blocks to incorporate score into your project!

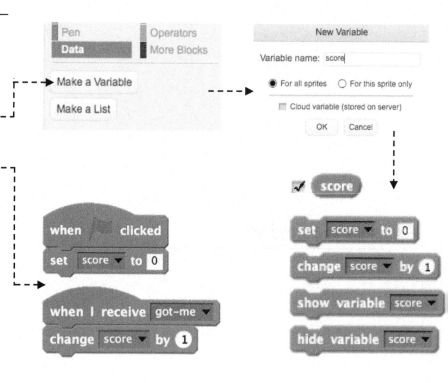

FEELING STUCK?

THAT'S OKAY! TRY THESE THINGS...

FINISHED?

- ☐ Not sure how to work with variables? Check out this project for more information: http://scratch.mit.edu/projects/2042755
- ☐ Or take a look at this video: http://youtu.be/uXq379XkhVw
- ☐ Explore and study code in games that use score to learn more about creating variables and incorporating score into a project.

- + Add your project to the Fish Chomp Remix studio: http://scratch.mit.edu/studios/475615
- + Challenge yourself to do more! How can you use score to add difficulty to your game design?
- + Find a game you are inspired by and remix it!

SCORE
REFLECTIONS

NAME:

RESPOND TO THE FOLLOWING REFLECTION PROMPTS USING THE SPACE PROVIDED BELOW OR IN YOUR DESIGN JOURNAL.

+ How would you explain variables to someone else?

+ What are variables good for?

EXTENSIONS

HOW CAN YOU EXTEND AND REIMAGINE GAMES IN SCRATCH?

Get into game design by adding extended features within your Scratch project! Choose at least one (or more!) of the following extensions and add it to your previously started maze, pong, or scrolling games.

START HERE

❑ Go to the Extensions studio:
   http://scratch.mit.edu/studios/475619

❑ Choose one (or more) of the extensions to explore.

❑ Incorporate your choice into your previously started game projects!

+ **SCORE** http://scratch.mit.edu/projects/1940443
Demonstrates how to set and change a score. Receive 10 points every time the Scratch cat is clicked.

+ **LEVELS** http://scratch.mit.edu/projects/1940453
Demonstrates how to change levels. Score increases by 1 every time the space bar is pressed. Level increases by 1 for every 10 points.

+ **TIMER** http://scratch.mit.edu/projects/1940445
Demonstrates how to use a timer. Use the mouse to navigate the Scratch cat to Gobo.

+ **ENEMIES** http://scratch.mit.edu/projects/1940450
Demonstrates how to add an enemy. Avoid the tennis ball by using the up and down arrow keys.

+ **REWARDS** http://scratch.mit.edu/projects/1940456
Demonstrates how to collect items. Use the arrow keys to move the Scratch cat around to collect quest items.

+ **MOUSE** http://scratch.mit.edu/projects/25192659
Demonstrates how to program the mouse to control game play. Move the mouse to move the paddle.

+ **RESTART** http://scratch.mit.edu/projects/25192935
Demonstrates how to make a button to restart the game. Click on the RESTART button to restart.

+ **MENU** http://scratch.mit.edu/projects/25192991
Demonstrates how to display a menu screen at the beginning of the game. Click START or DIRECTIONS on the menu screen.

+ **MULTIPLAYER** http://scratch.mit.edu/projects/25192711
Demonstrates how to add another player to the game. Player 1 uses the arrow keys to navigate Pico through the maze, and player 2 uses the W, A, S, D keys to navigate Nano through the maze.

THINGS TO TRY

+ The backpack can be an extremely useful tool while programming in Scratch. It can store everything from lines of code, to music files, to sprites, and more. Try using it to incorporate extensions into your game projects.

+ Alternatively, sketching out ideas and bits of code in your design journal is another great method for planning how to incorporate your extensions.

FINISHED?

+ Add another extension to your maze, pong, or scrolling game.
+ Challenge yourself to do more! Continue going through each of the extensions and add them to your games.
+ Help a neighbor!
+ Share your project with a neighbor and give each other feedback on your games.

EXTENSIONS REFLECTIONS

NAME:

RESPOND TO THE FOLLOWING REFLECTION PROMPTS USING THE SPACE PROVIDED BELOW OR IN YOUR DESIGN JOURNAL.

+ What are different ways of increasing difficulty in a game?

+ Which extensions did you add to your game project?

+ Describe your process for including the extension(s) in your game?

INTERACTIONS

WHAT DIFFERENTIATES A SCRATCH PROJECT FROM A STILL IMAGE OR A VIDEO?

Tackle these nine puzzles that engage some of the more advanced concepts in Scratch related to interactivity. Each of these challenges has several possible solutions.

START HERE

❑ Create a Scratch program for each of the nine interactivity puzzles.

❑ **PUZZLE 1:** Whenever you press the B key, the sprite gets a little bigger. Whenever you press the S key, the sprite gets a little smaller.

❑ **PUZZLE 2:** Whenever the sprite hears a loud sound, it changes color.

❑ **PUZZLE 3:** Whenever the sprite is in the top 25% of the screen, it says "I like it up here."

❑ **PUZZLE 4:** When the sprite touches something blue, it plays a high note. When the sprite touches something red, it plays a low note.

❑ **PUZZLE 5:** Whenever two sprites collide, one of them says: "Excuse me."

❑ **PUZZLE 6:** Whenever the cat sprite gets near the dog sprite, the dog turns and runs from the cat.

❑ **PUZZLE 7:** Whenever you click on the background, a flower appears at that spot.

❑ **PUZZLE 8:** Whenever you click on a sprite, all other sprites do a dance.

❑ **PUZZLE 9:** Whenever you move the mouse-pointer, the sprite follows but doesn't touch the mouse-pointer.

FEELING STUCK?

THAT'S OKAY! TRY THESE THINGS...

❑ Before getting started in Scratch, write down ideas in your design journal for possible ways of programming each of the interactivity puzzles.

❑ Work with a neighbor. Collaborating with a partner can be a great way to solve problems and gain new perspectives on ways of programming in Scratch!

FINISHED?

+ Add each of the projects you create to the Interaction Studio: http://scratch.mit.edu/studios/487213

+ Help a neighbor!

+ Discuss your strategies for approaching each puzzle with a partner. Take notes about the similarities and differences in your methods.

INTERACTIONS REFLECTIONS

NAME:

RESPOND TO THE FOLLOWING REFLECTION PROMPTS USING THE SPACE PROVIDED BELOW OR IN YOUR DESIGN JOURNAL.

+ Which puzzles did you work on?

+ What was your strategy for solving the puzzles?

+ Which puzzles helped you think about your game project?

DEBUG IT!

HELP! CAN YOU DEBUG THESE FIVE SCRATCH PROGRAMS?

In this activity, you will investigate what is going awry and find a solution for each of the five Debug It! challenges.

START HERE

❑ Go to the Unit 4 Debug It! Studio:
http://scratch.mit.edu/studios/475634/

❑ Test and debug each of the five debugging challenges in the studio.

❑ Write down your solution or remix the buggy program with your solution.

FEELING STUCK?

THAT'S OKAY! TRY THESE THINGS...

❑ Make a list of possible bugs in the program.
❑ Keep track of your work! This can be a useful reminder of what you have already tried and point you toward what to try next.
❑ Share and compare your problem finding and problem solving approaches with a neighbor until you find something that works for you!

❑ **DEBUG IT! 4.1** http://scratch.mit.edu/projects/24271192

In this project, the "Inventory" list should be updated every time Scratch Cat picks up a new item. But Scratch Cat can only pick up the laptop. How do we fix the program?

❑ **DEBUG IT! 4.2** http://scratch.mit.edu/projects/24271303

In this project, Scratch Cat gets 10 points for collecting Yellow Gobos and loses 10 points for colliding with Pink Gobos. But something isn't working. How do we fix the program?

❑ **DEBUG IT! 4.3** http://scratch.mit.edu/projects/24271446

In this project, Scratch Cat is thinking of a number between 1 and 10. But something is wrong with the guess checking – it doesn't work consistently. How do we fix the program?

❑ **DEBUG IT! 4.4** http://scratch.mit.edu/projects/24271475

In this project, the "# of hits" display should increase by 1 every time the Scratch Cat is hit by a tennis ball. But the "# of hits" increases by more than 1 when Scratch Cat is hit. How do we fix the program?

❑ **DEBUG IT! 4.5** http://scratch.mit.edu/projects/24271560

In this project, Scratch Cat is navigating a maze to get to the yellow rectangle. But Scratch Cat can walk through walls. How do we fix the program?

FINISHED?

+ Add code commentary by right clicking on blocks in your scripts. This can help others understand different parts of your program!
+ Discuss your testing and debugging practices with a partner. Make note of the similarities and differences in your strategies.
+ Help a neighbor!

DEBUG IT!
REFLECTIONS

NAME:

RESPOND TO THE FOLLOWING REFLECTION PROMPTS USING THE SPACE PROVIDED BELOW OR IN YOUR DESIGN JOURNAL.

+ What was the problem?

+ How did you identify the problem?

+ How did you fix the problem?

+ Did others have alternative approaches to fixing the problem?

UNIT 5
DIVING DEEPER

YOU ARE HERE

0   1   2   3   4   **5**   6

WHAT'S INCLUDED

KNOW WANT LEARN
ROUND TWO
ADVANCED CONCEPTS
HARDWARE & EXTENSIONS
ACTIVITY DESIGN
MY DEBUG IT!

KNOW WANT LEARN

NAME: _____

What do you know about creative computing & scratch? What do you want to know next? This activity is an opportunity for you to consider which areas of Scratch you feel comfortable navigating (What do I know?) and which areas you would like to explore further (What do I want to know?). Use different resources around you to investigate what you want to know, and then share your findings (What did I learn?).

WHAT DO I KNOW?

Reflecting on your design experiences so far, write down what you know about Scratch and creative computing.

WHAT DO I WANT TO KNOW?

Based on your personal interests, generate a list of things you want to find out more about or discover next.

WHAT DID I LEARN?

Gather resources to investigate items from the list you created above, and then share what you learned from your research.

KNOW WANT LEARN REFLECTIONS

NAME:

RESPOND TO THE FOLLOWING REFLECTION PROMPTS USING THE SPACE PROVIDED BELOW OR IN YOUR DESIGN JOURNAL.

+ What do you know?

+ What do you want to know?

+ What did you learn?

+ What were your strategies for investigating what you wanted to know?

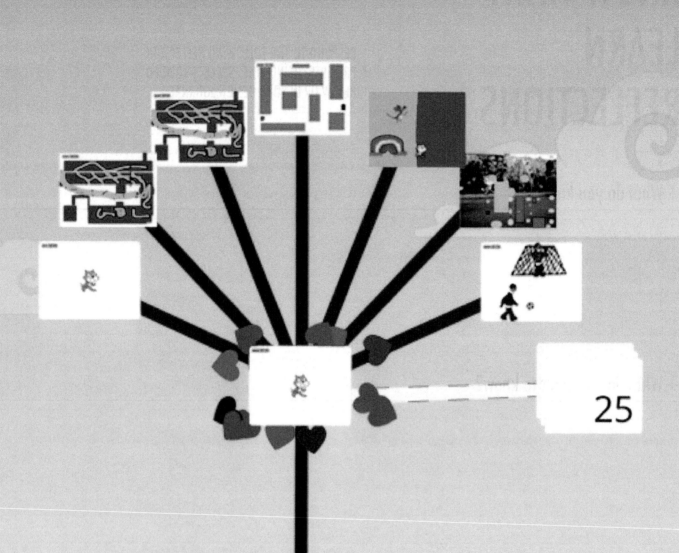

ROUND TWO REFLECTIONS

NAME:

RESPOND TO THE FOLLOWING REFLECTION PROMPTS USING THE SPACE PROVIDED BELOW OR IN YOUR DESIGN JOURNAL.

+ Why did you choose that project or activity to work on?

+ What would you do if you had more time?

VIDEO SENSING

HOW CAN YOU USE VIDEO SENSING IN YOUR SCRATCH PROJECTS?

Did you know that you can make your Scratch projects interactive through a webcam? Explore this advanced Scratch concept by creating a project that incorporates the video sensing feature. - - - - - →

START HERE

- ❏ Open an existing Scratch project or start a new project to add video sensing.
- ❏ Check out blocks for video sensing in the Sensing category. - - - - - - - - - - - - - - - - - - →
- ❏ Experiment with video on, turn video, and set video transparency to blocks to program your project to sense video motion. - - - - - - - - - - →

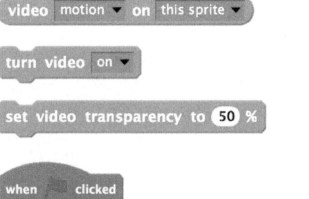

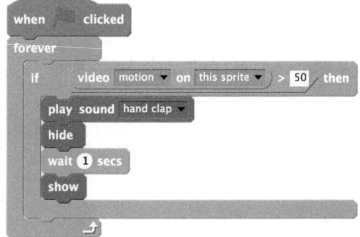

THINGS TO TRY

- ❏ Make sure your webcam is connected! Test it out using the turn video on block.
- ❏ If you're feeling a little stuck, that's okay! Explore some of the other projects in the Video Sensing studio to see how they use the video blocks or use the Tips Window to learn more about video sensing.

FINISHED?

- + Add your project to the Advanced Concepts studio: http://scratch.mit.edu/studios/221311
- + Add video sensing to one of your past projects!
- + Help a neighbor!
- + Remix a project in the Video Sensing studio.

CLONING

HOW CAN YOU USE CLONING IN YOUR
SCRATCH PROJECTS?

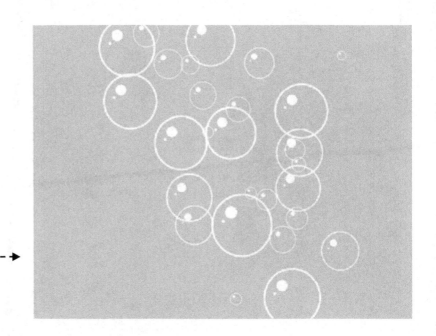

Cloning is an easy way to create multiples of the same sprite. You can use cloning to make many objects and create cool effects in a project.

Explore this advanced Scratch concept by creating a project that incorporates the cloning feature.

START HERE

❑ Open an existing Scratch project or start a new project to experiment with cloning.

❑ Check out blocks for cloning in the Control category.

❑ Experiment with the blocks to create clones of your sprite. Define behaviors for what your cloned sprites will do.

```
when I start as a clone
```

```
create clone of myself ▾
```

```
delete this clone
```

```
when ⚑ clicked
go to x: 206 y: 0
forever
    wait 0.5 secs
    create clone of myself ▾
```

```
when I start as a clone
forever
    repeat until touching edge ▾ ?
        change x by -5
        change ghost ▾ effect by 1.5
    delete this clone
```

THINGS TO TRY

❑ If you can't see your clone initially, check if the original sprite is in the same location – it might be covering the clone! Program your original sprite or the clone to move or go to different locations so you can see them.

❑ Stuck? That's okay! Explore some of the other projects in the Cloning Studio to see how they use cloning or search in the Tips Window to learn more about the Create Clone and When I start as a Clone blocks.

FINISHED?

+ Add your project to the Cloning studio: http://scratch.mit.edu/studios/201437
+ Add cloning to one of your past projects!
+ Help a neighbor!
+ Remix a project in the Cloning studio.

ADVANCED CONCEPTS REFLECTIONS

NAME:

RESPOND TO THE FOLLOWING REFLECTION PROMPTS USING THE SPACE PROVIDED BELOW OR IN YOUR DESIGN JOURNAL.

+ Which advanced concept(s) did you choose to explore?

+ What was your strategy for learning more about the concept(s) you selected?

HARDWARE & EXTENSIONS REFLECTIONS

NAME:

RESPOND TO THE FOLLOWING REFLECTION PROMPTS USING THE SPACE PROVIDED BELOW OR IN YOUR DESIGN JOURNAL.

+ Which hardware or extension did you explore?

+ How did you incorporate the digital and the physical?

+ What was difficult?

+ What was surprising?

ACTIVITY DESIGN

NAME: _____

How can you help others learn more about Scratch and creative computing? Design an activity that helps other people learn Scratch. It can be an off-computer activity (like Creature Construction), project idea (like Build-a-Band), or challenge activity (like Debug It!). You could even develop a new type of activity or handout! Brainstorm using the questions below, and then use the activity and handout planners to give more detail.

WHO IS THIS FOR?

Who is your audience? Who do you want to help learn more about Scratch and creative computing?

WHAT WILL THEY LEARN?

What are the learning goals? What new things do you hope people will learn from using your activity?

WHAT DO THEY NEED?

What supplies will people need? What other types of support will help people successfully engage in your activity?

(TITLE)

SUGGESTED TIME
__-__ MINUTES

OBJECTIVES   (2 LEARNING GOALS)
By completing this activity, learners will:
+

+

ACTIVITY DESCRIPTION

(PROJECT INSTRUCTIONS)
❏ What will learners create? How will they do this?

❏ How will learners share their work with others?

❏ How will learners reflect on their designs?

RESOURCES

(2 PROJECT RESOURCES - studios, handouts, etc.)
❏

❏

REFLECTION PROMPTS

(3 REFLECTION QUESTIONS)
+

+

+

REVIEWING STUDENT WORK

(2 WAYS TO CHECK IF A LEARNER COMPLETED THE ACTIVITY)
+

+

NOTES

(TIPS AND TRICKS)
+

+

+

NOTES TO SELF

❏ --------------------------------

❏ --------------------------------

❏ --------------------------------

❏ --------------------------------

(TITLE)

(PROJECT OVERVIEW)

(PROJECT PICTURE)

(PROJECT DESCRIPTION)

START HERE

(PROJECT INSTRUCTIONS)

❑

❑

❑

❑

(ILLUSTRATED PROJECT INSTRUCTIONS)

THINGS TO TRY

FINISHED?

(3 THINGS TO DO IF THEY GET STUCK)

❑

❑

❑

(3 THINGS TO DO IF THEY HAVE EXTRA TIME)

+

+

+

ACTIVITY DESIGN REFLECTIONS

NAME:

RESPOND TO THE FOLLOWING REFLECTION PROMPTS USING THE SPACE PROVIDED BELOW OR IN YOUR DESIGN JOURNAL.

+ Who do you envision using your activity or resource?

+ What do you hope people will learn from using your activity or resource?

+ What challenges might learners experience in doing the activity or using the resource? How might you further support them in dealing with these challenges?

MY DEBUG IT!

Hmm...

IT'S TIME TO DESIGN YOUR OWN DEBUG IT PROGRAM. WHAT WILL YOU CREATE?

In this activity, you will create your own Debug It! challenge for others to investigate, solve, and remix.

START HERE

- ❏ Reflect back on the different kinds of bugs you've encountered in creating and debugging your own projects.
- ❏ Generate a list of possible debugging challenges you could create. A Debug It! can focus on a specific concept, block, interaction, or some other programming challenge.
- ❏ Build your Debug It! program.

PLANS FOR MY DEBUG IT!

NOTES TO SELF

- ❏ ....
- ❏ ....
- ❏ ....
- ❏ ....
- ❏ ....

FINISHED?

- + Add your debugging challenge to the My Debug It! studio: http://scratch.mit.edu/studios/475637
- + Swap Debug It! programs with a neighbor and try to solve each other's buggy programs.
- + Help a neighbor.
- + Try debugging other programs in the My Debug It! studio.

MY DEBUG IT! REFLECTIONS

NAME:

RESPOND TO THE FOLLOWING REFLECTION PROMPTS USING THE SPACE PROVIDED BELOW OR IN YOUR DESIGN JOURNAL.

+ What was the problem?

+ Where did your inspiration come from?

+ How did you imagine others investigating and solving the challenge?

+ Did others have alternative approaches to finding and fixing the problem than what you expected? What were their strategies?

UNIT 6
HACKATHON

YOU ARE HERE

0 0 1 2 3 4 5 6

WHAT'S INCLUDED

PROJECT PITCH
PROJECT PLANNING
DESIGN SPRINT
PROJECT FEEDBACK
PROJECT CHECK-IN
UNFOCUS GROUP

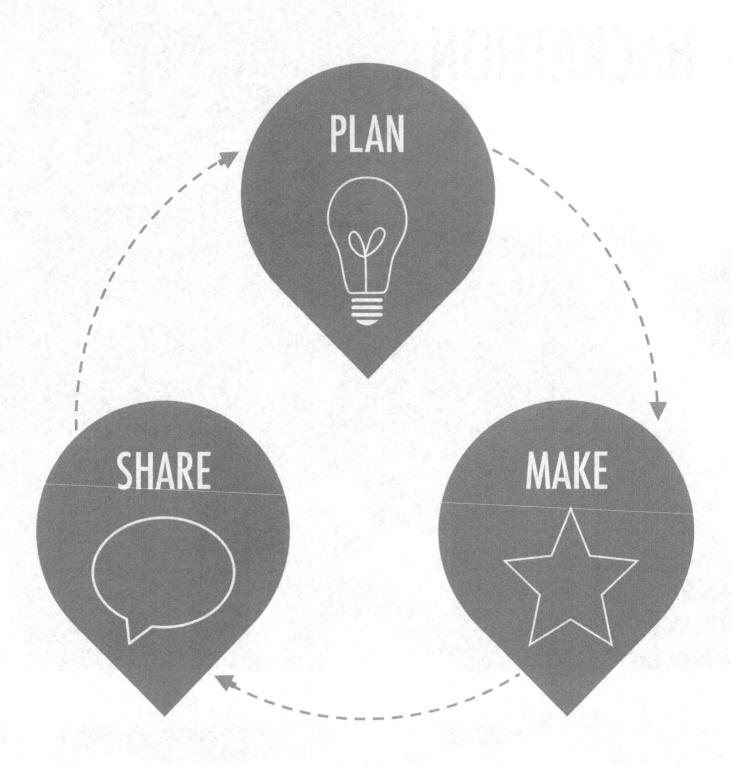

PROJECT PITCH

Use the prompts below to brainstorm ideas for projects you're interested in working on during the hackathon. You will have 30 seconds to pitch your ideas, interests, and skills to the rest of the group!

MY FAVORITE PROJECT

What has been your favorite project to work on so far? What made this project stand out for you?

MY HACKATHON PROJECT IDEA

What kinds of projects are you interested in creating next?

MY SKILLS AND INTERESTS

What knowledge, skills, or talents would you like to contribute to a project?

PROJECT PLANNING

Use the prompts below to start thinking about the elements needed to develop your project.

MY PROJECT

Describe the project you want to create.

List the steps needed in order to create your project.

MY RESOURCES

What resources (e.g., people, sample projects) do you already have?

What resources (e.g., people, sample projects) might you need to develop your project?

PROJECT SKETCHES

PROJECT SKETCHES BY: _____

Use the space below to draw sketches of what your project will look like!

MY PROJECT SKETCHES

What's happening? What are the important elements?

What's happening? What are the important elements?

What's happening? What are the important elements?

What's happening? What are the important elements?

DESIGN SPRINT REFLECTIONS

NAME:

RESPOND TO THE FOLLOWING REFLECTION PROMPTS USING THE SPACE PROVIDED BELOW OR IN YOUR DESIGN JOURNAL.

+ What part of your project will you be working on today?

+ What might you need help with in order to make progress?

PROJECT FEEDBACK

FEEDBACK FOR: _____

PROJECT TITLE: _____

RED, YELLOW, GREEN

FEEDBACK BY	[RED] What is something that doesn't work or could be improved?	[YELLOW] What is something that is confusing or could be done differently?	[GREEN] What is something that works well or you really like about the project?

PARTS OF THE PROJECT THAT MIGHT BE HELPFUL TO THINK ABOUT:

+ Clarity: Did you understand what the project is supposed to do?
+ Features: What features does the project have? Does the project work as expected?
+ Appeal: How engaging is the project? Is it interactive, original, sophisticated, funny, or interesting? How did you feel as you interacted with it?

PROJECT FEEDBACK REFLECTIONS

NAME:

RESPOND TO THE FOLLOWING REFLECTION PROMPTS USING THE SPACE PROVIDED BELOW OR IN YOUR DESIGN JOURNAL.

+ What aspects of your project could someone give you feedback about?

+ What feedback, if any, do you plan to incorporate into your project next?

PROJECT CHECK-IN

CHECK-IN BY: _____

Discuss your design progress with your team and outline a plan for next steps based on feedback.

PROJECT PROGRESS

What has been your favorite part of the process so far?

What parts of your project still need to be worked on?

NEXT STEPS

What parts of your project will each group member be working on next?

What might you need help with in order to make progress?

UNFOCUS GROUP

In this activity, you will interview and observe others to get feedback on your project-in-progress.

IDENTIFY

+ What kinds of people might be able to offer you a unique perspective on your project?

+ Who are two unfocus group members you plan to share your project draft with?

OBSERVE

Share your project with your unfocus group and observe their reactions.

+ What are they getting stuck on?

+ Are they interacting with your project the way you imagined?

+ Are they doing anything surprising?

INTERVIEW

After you observe, interview your group about their experience.

+ What feedback did you receive from your interview?

+ What suggestions, if any, do you plan to incorporate into your project next?

UNFOCUS GROUP REFLECTIONS

NAME:

RESPOND TO THE FOLLOWING REFLECTION PROMPTS USING THE SPACE PROVIDED BELOW OR IN YOUR DESIGN JOURNAL.

+ Describe your unfocus group participants and why you chose them.

+ How might their ideas influence your project?

PROJECT REFLECTIONS

PROJECT REFLECTIONS BY: _____

Use the prompts below to reflect on your design process.

WHAT?

What is your project?
How does it work? How did you come up with the idea?

SO WHAT?

What was your process for developing the project?
What was interesting, challenging, and surprising? Why?
What did you learn?

NOW WHAT?

What are you most proud of about your project?
What would you change?

WHAT DO YOU WANT TO CREATE NEXT?

SHOWCASE REFLECTIONS

NAME:

RESPOND TO THE FOLLOWING REFLECTION PROMPTS USING THE SPACE PROVIDED BELOW OR IN YOUR DESIGN JOURNAL.

+ Look through your design notebook. What types of notes did you take?

+ Which notes were most helpful?

+ What has been your favorite Scratch project to work on so far? Why is it your favorite?

+ What do you want to create next?

APPENDIX

GLOSSARY

A guide to key words, concepts, and practices:

Visit the Scratch help pages at http://scratch.mit.edu/help or the community-generated Scratch Wiki at http://wiki.scratch.mit.edu for additional, Scratch-specific terminology.

abstracting and modularizing: The computational practice of exploring connections between the whole and the parts.

animation: An illusion of continuous motion created by the rapid display of a sequence of still images with incremental differences.

backdrop: One out of possibly many frames, or backgrounds, of the Stage.

backpack: A Scratch feature that can be used to conveniently transfer media and/or scripts between projects.

bitmap: An image that is defined by a two-dimensional array (grid) of discrete color values (a.k.a. "pixels"). Contrast with vector graphics.

broadcast: A message that is sent through the Scratch program, activating receiving scripts.

cloning: A Scratch feature that allows a sprite to create duplicates of itself while the project is running.

computational concepts: The concepts designers engage with as they program, such as sequence, loops, conditionals, events, parallelism, operators, and data.

computational perspectives: The broader perspectives that designers may form about world around them through computing – such as expressing themselves, connecting with others, and posing questions about technology's role in the world.

computational practices: The distinctive habits of mind that programmers develop as they work, such as experimenting and iterating, testing and debugging, remixing and reusing work, and abstracting and modularizing.

conditionals: The computational concept of making decisions based on conditions (e.g., current variable values).

control: One of the ten categories of Scratch blocks. They are color-coded gold, and are used to control scripts.

costume: One out of possibly many "frames" or alternate appearances of a sprite. A sprite can change its look to any of its costumes.

critique group: A group of designers who share ideas and test projects-in-progress with one another in order to get feedback on how to further develop their projects.

data: The computational concept of storing, retrieving, and updating values.

design sprint: A specified amount of time dedicated to working intensely on developing projects.

events: The computational concept of one thing causing another thing to happen.

experimenting and iterating: The computational practice of developing a little bit, then trying it out, then developing some more.

hardware and extensions: Supplemental materials that connect the digital world of Scratch with the physical world. Examples of hardware extensions include: LEGO WeDo, PicoBoard, and MaKey MaKey.

interactive collage: A Scratch project that incorporates a variety of clickable sprites.

looks: One of the ten categories of Scratch blocks. They are color-coded purple, and are used to control a sprite's appearance.

loops: The computational concept of running the same sequence multiple times.

make a block: A feature found within the More Blocks category that allows students to create and define their own custom block or procedure.

motion: One of the ten categories of Scratch blocks. They are color-coded medium-blue, and are used to control a sprite's movement.

operators: The computational concept of supporting mathematical and logical expressions.

paint editor: Scratch's built-in image editor. Many Scratchers create their own sprites, costumes, and backdrops using it.

parallelism: The computational concept of making things happen at the same time.

pass-it-on story: A Scratch project that is started by a pair of people, and then passed on to two other pairs to extend and reimagine.

pitch: An activity in which students either announce a project idea in order to recruit other team members, or promote their interests, skills, and talents in order to be recruited by other teams.

presentation mode: A display mode in Scratch that allows projects to be viewed at an enlarged size. It is accessed by pressing the button on the top left of the Scratch program. This mode is also called full screen mode or enlarged screen.

profile page: A page on the Scratch online community dedicated to displaying information about a Scratch user, such as projects they have created or bookmarked (a.k.a. "favorited").

project editor: A feature of the Scratch online community that allows projects to be modified. This includes the script area (where scripts are assembled), the sprite area (where sprites can be manipulated), and the stage area (where sprites are positioned and where backgrounds can be accessed).

red, yellow, green: A reflection and sharing activity in which individuals identify aspects of their projects as not going well or still needing work ("red"), confusing or contentious ("yellow"), or working well ("green").

remix: A creative work that is derived from an original work (or from another remix). A remix typically introduces new content or stylistic elements, while retaining a degree of similarity to the original work.

reusing and remixing: The computational practice of making something by building on existing projects or ideas.

scripts: One or more Scratch blocks connected together to form a sequence. Scripts begin with an event block that responds to input (e.g., mouse click, broadcast). When triggered, additional blocks connected to the event block are executed one at a time.

sensing: One of the ten categories of Scratch blocks. They are color-coded light-blue, and are used to detect different forms of input (e.g., mouse position) or program state (e.g., sprite position).

sequence: The computational concept of identifying a series of steps for a task.

showcase: A strategy for sharing in which students present their final projects to others and reflect on their design processes and computational creation experiences.

sound: An audio file that can be played in a Scratch project, available by importing from Scratch's built-in sound library, or creating a new recording. Sounds are played by using sound blocks, which control a sound's volume, tempo, and more.

sprite: A media object that performs actions on the stage in a Scratch project.

stage: The background of a Scratch project. The stage can have scripts, backdrops (costumes), and sounds, similar to a sprite.

studio: A user-created gallery in the Scratch online community that can be used to highlight projects contributed by one or many users.

testing and debugging: The computational practice of making sure things work – and finding and solving problems when they arise.

tips window: Built directly into the Project Editor, the Tips Window is a form of getting help in Scratch.

unfocus group: An activity in which students share their projects-in-progress and request feedback from a diverse collection of people.

variables and lists: A changeable value or collection of values recorded in Scratch's memory. Variables can store one value at a time, while lists can store multiple values.

vector graphic: An image that is defined by a collection of geometric shapes (e.g., circles, rectangles) and colors. Contrast with bitmap.

video sensing: A Scratch feature that makes use of video from a webcam to detect motion or display video input on the stage.

LINKS

A summary of links to resources:

TYPE	DESCRIPTION	LINK
Website	Scratch	http://scratch.mit.edu
Website	ScratchEd	http://scratch-ed.org
Website	Flash	http://helpx.adobe.com/flash-player.html
Resource	Offline Version of Scratch	http://scratch.mit.edu/scratch2download
Resource	Scratch Cards	http://scratch.mit.edu/help/cards
Resource	Scratch Community Guidelines	http://scratch.mit.edu/community_guidelines
Resource	Scratch Remix FAQ	http://scratch.mit.edu/help/faq/#remix
Resource	Scratch Wiki	http://wiki.scratch.mit.edu
Resource	Scratch Discussion Forums	http://scratch.mit.edu/discuss
Resource	Scratch FAQ	http://scratch.mit.edu/help/faq
Resource	LEGO WeDo Construction Set	http://bit.ly/LEGOWeDo
Resource	MaKey MaKey	http://makeymakey.com
Resource	PicoBoard	https://www.sparkfun.com/products/10311
Resource	*Scratch Design Studio* Studio List	http://scratch.mit.edu/users/ScratchDesignStudio/studios
Video	Scratch Overview Video	http://vimeo.com/65583694 http://youtu.be/-SjuiawRMU4
Video	Unit 1 *Programmed to Dance* Videos	http://vimeo.com/28612347 http://vimeo.com/28612585 http://vimeo.com/28612800 http://vimeo.com/28612970
Video	*Backpack* Video Tutorial	http://bit.ly/scratchbackpack
Video	*Make a Block* Video Tutorial	http://bit.ly/makeablock
Video	*Variables* Video Tutorial	http://bit.ly/scratchvariables
Video	*How can I connect Scratch with other technologies?* Video Playlist	http://bit.ly/hardwareandextensions
Video	Scratch Chain Reaction Video	http://bit.ly/ScratchChainReaction
Studio	Unit 0 *Scratch Surprise* Studio	http://scratch.mit.edu/studios/460431
Studio	Unit 0 *Sample Projects* Studio	http://scratch.mit.edu/studios/137903

TYPE	DESCRIPTION	LINK
Studio	Unit 1 *About Me* Studio	http://scratch.mit.edu/studios/475470
Studio	Unit 1 *Step-by-Step* Studio	http://scratch.mit.edu/studios/475476
Studio	Unit 1 *10 Blocks* Studio	http://scratch.mit.edu/studios/475480
Studio	Unit 1 Example Studios	http://scratch.mit.edu/studios/211580 http://scratch.mit.edu/studios/138296 http://scratch.mit.edu/studios/138297 http://scratch.mit.edu/studios/138298
Studio	Unit 1 *Debug It!* Studio	http://scratch.mit.edu/studios/475483
Studio	Unit 2 *Music Video* Studio	http://scratch.mit.edu/studios/475517
Studio	Unit 2 *Build-a-Band* Studio	http://scratch.mit.edu/studios/475523
Studio	Unit 2 *Orange Square, Purple Circle* Studio	http://scratch.mit.edu/studios/475527
Studio	Unit 2 *It's Alive!* Studio	http://scratch.mit.edu/studios/475529
Studio	*Unit 2 Debug It!* Studio	http://scratch.mit.edu/studios/475539
Studio	Unit 3 *Pass It On* Studio	http://scratch.mit.edu/studios/475543
Studio	Unit 3 *Characters* Studio	http://scratch.mit.edu/studios/475545
Studio	Unit 3 *Conversations* Studio	http://scratch.mit.edu/studios/475547
Studio	Unit 3 *Broadcast Examples* studio	http://scratch.mit.edu/studios/202853
Studio	Unit 3 *Scenes* Studio	http://scratch.mit.edu/studios/475550
Studio	Unit 3 *Debug It!* Studio	http://scratch.mit.edu/studios/475554
Studio	Unit 4 *Games* Studio	http://scratch.mit.edu/studios/487504
Studio	Unit 4 *Score Examples* Studio	http://scratch.mit.edu/studios/218313
Studio	Unit 4 *Fish Chomp Remix* Studio	http://scratch.mit.edu/studios/475615
Studio	Unit 4 *Extensions* Studio	http://scratch.mit.edu/studios/452336
Studio	Unit 4 *Interactions* Studio	http://scratch.mit.edu/studios/487213
Studio	Unit 4 *Debug It!* Studio	http://scratch.mit.edu/studios/475634
Studio	Unit 5 *Advanced Concepts* Studio	http://scratch.mit.edu/studios/221311
Studio	Unit 5 *Video Sensing Examples* Studio	http://scratch.mit.edu/studios/201435
Studio	Unit 5 *Cloning Examples* Studio	http://scratch.mit.edu/studios/201437
Studio	Unit 5 *My Debug It!* Studio	http://scratch.mit.edu/studios/475637
Studio	Unit 6 *Hackathon* Studio	http://scratch.mit.edu/studios/488267
Project	Unit 1 Debug It! 1.1	http://scratch.mit.edu/projects/10437040

TYPE	DESCRIPTION	LINK
Project	Unit 1 Debug It! 1.2	http://scratch.mit.edu/projects/10437249
Project	Unit 1 Debug It! 1.3	http://scratch.mit.edu/projects/10437366
Project	Unit 1 Debug It! 1.4	http://scratch.mit.edu/projects/10437439
Project	Unit 1 Debug It! 1.5	http://scratch.mit.edu/projects/10437476
Project	Unit 2 Debug It! 2.1	http://scratch.mit.edu/projects/23266426
Project	Unit 2 Debug It! 2.2	http://scratch.mit.edu/projects/24268476
Project	Unit 2 Debug It! 2.3	http://scratch.mit.edu/projects/24268506
Project	Unit 2 Debug It! 2.4	http://scratch.mit.edu/projects/23267140
Project	Unit 2 Debug It! 2.5	http://scratch.mit.edu/projects/23267245
Project	Unit 3 *Penguin Joke* Starter Project	http://scratch.mit.edu/projects/10015800
Project	Unit 3 Debug It! 3.1	http://scratch.mit.edu/projects/24269007
Project	Unit 3 Debug It! 3.2	http://scratch.mit.edu/projects/24269046
Project	Unit 3 Debug It! 3.3	http://scratch.mit.edu/projects/24269070
Project	Unit 3 Debug It! 3.4	http://scratch.mit.edu/projects/24269097
Project	Unit 3 Debug It! 3.5	http://scratch.mit.edu/projects/24269131
Project	Unit 4 *Maze* Starter Project	http://scratch.mit.edu/projects/24788382
Project	Unit 4 *Pong* Starter Project	http://scratch.mit.edu/projects/10128515
Project	Unit 4 *Scrolling* Starter Project	http://scratch.mit.edu/projects/22162012
Project	Unit 4 *Fish Chomp* Starter Project	http://scratch.mit.edu/projects/10859244
Project	Unit 4 *Extensions: Variables* Example Project	http://scratch.mit.edu/projects/2042755
Project	Unit 4 *Extensions: Score* Example Project	http://scratch.mit.edu/projects/1940443
Project	Unit 4 *Extensions: Levels* Example Project	http://scratch.mit.edu/projects/1940453
Project	Unit 4 *Extensions: Enemies* Example Project	http://scratch.mit.edu/projects/1940450
Project	Unit 4 *Extensions: Rewards* Example Project	http://scratch.mit.edu/projects/1940456
Project	Unit 4 *Extensions: Timer* Example Project	http://scratch.mit.edu/projects/1940445
Project	Unit 4 *Extensions: Mouse* Example Project	http://scratch.mit.edu/projects/25192659
Project	Unit 4 *Extensions: Multi-Player* Example Project	http://scratch.mit.edu/projects/25192711
Project	Unit 4 *Extensions: Restart* Example Project	http://scratch.mit.edu/projects/25192935
Project	Unit 4 *Extensions: Menu* Example Project	http://scratch.mit.edu/projects/25192991
Project	Unit 4 Debug It! 4.1	http://scratch.mit.edu/projects/24271192

TYPE	DESCRIPTION	LINK
Project	Unit 4 Debug It! 4.2	http://scratch.mit.edu/projects/24271303
Project	Unit 4 Debug It! 4.3	http://scratch.mit.edu/projects/24271446
Project	Unit 4 Debug It! 4.4	http://scratch.mit.edu/projects/24271475
Project	Unit 4 Debug It! 4.5	http://scratch.mit.edu/projects/24271560

CPSIA information can be obtained
at www.ICGtesting.com
Printed in the USA
LVOW03s1109130816
500247LV00015B/272/P

9 781503 388079